THE LIBRARY OF HIP-HOP BIOGRAPHIES™

LL Cool J

Rich Juzwiak

The Rosen Publishing Group, Inc., New York

Published in 2006 by The Rosen Publishing Group, Inc.
29 East 21st Street, New York, NY 10010

Copyright © 2006 by The Rosen Publishing Group, Inc.

First Edition

Library of Congress Cataloging-in-Publication Data

Juzwiak, Richard.
LL Cool J/By Rich Juzwiak. — 1st ed.
    p. cm. — (The library of hip-hop biographies)
Includes bibliographical references and index.
ISBN 1-4042-0517-9 (library binding)
1. L. L. Cool J, 1968 — Juvenile literature. 2. Rap musicians — United States — Biography — Juvenile literature. I. Title. II. Series.

ML3930.L115J89 2006
782.421649'092 — dc22

2005021326

Manufactured in the United States of America

On the cover: LL Cool J performs at the BET Comedy Awards at the Pasadena Civic Center in Pasadena, California, on September 28, 2004.

CONTENTS

INTRODUCTION

Rapper, actor, spokesman, entrepreneur, philanthropist, husband, father, icon: these words are among many that describe the man the world knows as LL Cool J. Throughout his more than twenty years of fame, LL has worn many hats, both literally, as a headgear enthusiast—his hat collection is said to exceed 2,000 pieces—and figuratively, as an all-around entertainer. LL's rise to fame hasn't been easy. He has beat the odds by overcoming a turbulent childhood. Moreover, the rapper who helped bring hip-hop to the mainstream with hits like "I Need Love" and "I'm the Type of Guy," has remained relevant (and profitable) in the ever-changing world of popular music.

With eleven albums and more than 20 million records sold, LL is one of the most successful rappers of all time. Release after release, he has remained on top of his game with his quick-witted lyrics, infectious personality, and savvy

choices of musical collaborators, including such hip-hop heavy-weights as Rick Rubin, Marley Marl, the Neptunes, and Timbaland.

In this book, we'll examine how LL got his start. We'll travel through the highs and lows of his career and personal life. We'll ultimately reach an understanding of his success and the person behind it, who once dubbed himself the "greatest of all time."

CHAPTER ONE

BORN TO RHYME

LL Cool J was born James Todd Smith on January 14, 1968, in a Bayshore hospital, not far from the small house in Brentwood on New York's Long Island, where he would spend his first year with his parents, James and Ondrea Smith. Both nurses' aides, the Smiths put their only child on a path to music appreciation. LL's father was a former songwriter and keyboardist who briefly ran his own record label. His mother was a music enthusiast, whose soul records LL Cool J recalls listening to in the Bayshore, Long Island, home where the family soon relocated.

But it was LL's maternal grandfather's great love of music that left the biggest impression on the future rapper. Like LL's father, Eugene Griffith had a musical background (he played the saxophone). Like LL's mother, Eugene's record collection was extensive, and his jazz albums exposed LL to the likes of Duke Ellington, Billie Holliday, Miles Davis, and Wes Montgomery. "He opened the door of music to me," LL told *Essence* magazine in 1996. "Seeing someone I idolized love music so much made me love it, too."

LL soaked in the sounds during frequent trips to his maternal grandparents' house in Queens, which he would come to consider his hometown. He spent most of his boyhood summers in that house, bonding with Eugene and his grandmother, Ellen Griffith, a small but feisty woman who would eventually have a major influence on LL's rap career. Ellen instilled the faith that LL still talks about today. He attended a local church with his grandmother and cut his musical teeth by singing in its chorus (he eventually sang for Pope John Paul II with the St. Bonaventure Choir at New York's Shea Stadium in 1979).

LL and his mother moved in with his grandparents full-time when he was four years old. Broken down by her strained relationship with her husband, whom LL refers to as a "straight-up Dr. Jeckyll and Mr. Hyde" in his 1997 autobiography, *I Make My Own Rules*, Ondrea sought refuge in the Queens house. Their conflict soon came to a head when LL's father showed up at the house and, in a heated battle the four-year-old LL witnessed, shot Ondrea in the stomach and Eugene in the back.

Both survived the incident. Despite this violent attack, LL's mother refused to cooperate in the prosecution of his father, who fled to California and changed his name.

Doctors feared LL's mother would never walk again, but she eventually did with the help of a physical therapist, a man LL identifies only as Roscoe. LL's mother and Roscoe formed a romantic relationship and, along with LL, moved into a house in Long Island's North Babylon. While Ondrea worked two jobs, LL spent most of his days with Roscoe, who he says physically and emotionally abused him. LL was able to escape the abuse via weekend visits to his grandparents' house and at the home of his neighbors, the McCulloughs. The McCulloughs' house was full of foster kids, so even as an outsider, LL felt as if part of the family.

The McCulloughs' was not only a safe haven, it was also a place of musical creativity. There, LL and one of the troubled children the McCulloughs took in, Kenny, dubbed themselves Silver Streak (LL) and Solid Gold (Kenny). They mimicked hip-hop tapes of early rap stars such as Kurtis Blow, Grandmaster Flash, and the Furious Five. It was with Kenny that LL began experimenting with what would become the love of his creative life: rapping.

THE POWER OF THE RHYME

At age eleven, LL wanted nothing more than a dirt bike. Despite his begging, his grandparents refused to buy him one out of fear for his safety. Instead, they invested $2,000 in a DJ setup, presenting LL with a pair of turntables, a mixer, and a microphone.

The Sugar Hill Gang was the first hip-hop act to score a major hit. The success of its 1979 single "Rapper's Delight" convinced many up-and-coming DJs that a serious living could be made with this new style of music. Although the Sugar Hill Gang was virtually unknown at the time it recorded the song, its members are now widely regarded as hip-hop pioneers. The band is pictured here during a live performance at an unidentified location around 1979. Its members are, from left to right, Wonder Mike, Master Gee, and Big Bank Hank.

Also around this time, LL and his mother attended a concert featuring rap pioneers the Sugar Hill Gang. Both the turntables and the show kicked LL's involvement with hip-hop into high gear. The preteen initially hated the way his recorded nasal voice sounded, but LL soon felt empowered through rhyme. "For the first time in my life, I had power," he writes in *I Make My Own Rules*. "I could say anything I wanted and not be afraid. I could be as powerful as I always wanted to be."

LL was ready to take his power to the streets. At age twelve, he started hassling Jay Philpot, a Queens DJ, to allow him to perform in one of Philpot's gigs. Though Philpot initially brushed off the precocious boy, he finally agreed to let LL rap with him at a neighborhood block party. LL was so eager to perform that when problems with equipment delayed Philpot's set, he found a nearby DJ who gave him a chance to rock the mic. He immediately won over the crowd and showed Philpot his potential. Though Philpot was irritated that LL had deserted him at the party for another DJ, he soon enlisted the young rapper to accompany him to performances at various house and basement parties.

With a DJ providing his beats, a heaping dose of personality, and a lot of rhymes, LL was missing just one thing: a unique name. Up to this point, James Todd Smith had performed under the moniker J-Ski, inspired by the names of many other popular performers at that time, such as Luvbug Starski, Busy Bee-Starski, and Mike-ski. He settled on the name Cool J, reasoning that the word "cool" would never go out of style. When he told friend Playboy Mikey D about his new name, Mikey suggested he spruce it up by putting "Ladies Love" in front of it. LL agreed, the name stuck, and Ladies Love Cool James was born.

BEAT ELEVATES, THE SCRATCH EXCELS

LL began sending out demo tapes created with the turntables, mixer, and microphone his grandparents had given him. He sent the tapes to the address of every rap label he could find. But

RAP'S EARLY DAYS

Before rap became the popular music that it is today, it was an underground art form on the streets of large cities. It all started in the Bronx, New York, in 1974, when DJ Kool Herc experimented with records on two turntables before an audience. Herc switched back and forth (or "cut") between the stripped-down, drum-heavy midsections (or "breaks") of funk and soul hits. The technique soon caught on and DJs became an attraction of neighborhood block parties, where b-boys would break dance to the music. As DJing become more sophisticated, scratching (or manipulating a record back and forth under the needle to create rhythmic noise) and vocalists were added. Instead of singing over the music provided by the DJ, the vocalist spoke in a staccato manner that soon became known as rapping. Early on, the rapper's main function was to entice the crowd into dancing. But with each new MC (another word for "rapper" and short for "master of ceremony") that popped up came a sense of competition. Soon, rappers were "battling" with each other by bragging about their superior lyrics and delivery (or "flow"). Though today's hip-hop sounds very different from that of the 1970s and early 1980s, many of its early elements—sampling, bragging, and feuding—are still present.

soon, he found himself frustrated by the lack of response. Just as he was ready to give up, his mother bought him a drum machine. This allowed LL to create his own beats and not just rely on those found in his record collection.

Rick Rubin *(right)* is with LL Cool J at an MTV Aids fund-raiser in Rancho Palos Verdes, California, in 1997. Rubin was the main architect of the early Def Jam sound. Rubin, who cofounded the label with Russell Simmons, spiced up the hip-hop recordings of artists such as LL Cool J and the Beastie Boys with furious heavy metal guitar riffs. This blending of genres inspired a new form of hip-hop that later became known as metal rap.

With a sense of restored hope, LL sent out a new batch of demos with fresh beats. He contacted Rick Rubin, then a senior at New York University, who had produced T-La Rock and Jazzy Jay's minor hit "It's Yours." Sensing that Rubin was his only hope, the fifteen-year-old rapper began calling Rubin every day to check if he received the demo. Rubin ignored LL until one day, when schoolmate Adam Horowitz (who later came to be known as the Beastie Boys' Adrock) was in Rubin's "office" (in reality, his NYU dorm room), going through the piles of demo tapes Rubin had received from hopeful rappers. Impressed by LL's talent, Ad-Rock brought the tape to Rubin's attention, and Rubin contacted LL for a meeting.

LL met Rubin at his dorm and the pair began work on a more polished track they called "Catch This Break." They took that tape to Russell Simmons, the manager and producer who would soon cofound Def Jam Records with Rubin. Simmons wasn't impressed with the initial offering, but that didn't deter Rubin or LL. The pair headed to a proper studio to cut yet another demo. LL called on Jay Philpot to perform the scratching on the track, forming a bond with Philpot that has lasted throughout the rapper's career. LL even consulted his grandmother for advice on the song. (She told him to turn up the bass.)

"I Need a Beat," the product of this endeavor, immediately won over Simmons, who made the ode to hip-hop Def Jam's first release. The song, which cost $700 to make, was an overnight sensation, selling 100,000 copies soon after it hit the streets in the fall of 1984. With Jay Philpot (now known as Cut Creator) as his DJ, LL made a series of well-received promotional appearances. Encouraged by the response, Simmons commissioned a full album from LL, signing him to the label that the rapper continues to call home.

CHAPTER TWO

INSTANT SUCCESS

LL Cool J's career was on track with the Def Jam deal, which gave him the opportunity to have his music heard on a national level. However, during the making of his debut album, *Radio*, LL's personal life felt a crushing blow with the death of his grandfather. Though Eugene Griffith had survived the shots he sustained at the hand of LL's father, he never fully recovered and finally succumbed. His grandfather's passing put LL in a deep depression, though it did not stop him from completing the album. "I just took all the pain and channeled my energy into something

else," LL told VH1 in 2004. "Just focusing on my dream instead of letting myself be destroyed by it."

LL was so focused on his career that he dropped out of high school at age sixteen. Disappointed, his grandmother threw him out of the house. LL ended up homeless for two weeks until his manager, Cornell Clark, found out and offered his couch. (LL would later move back in with his grandmother.)

If LL spent some time hungry during this period, it wasn't for long. He soon received a $50,000 advance for *Radio*. Though LL went through the money quickly, he invested at least some of it wisely, buying the clothes, chains, and, especially, hats that would define his streetwise image. It would be years before the public saw LL without a hat on his head. ("Mentally, I wasn't right until I had on my hat," he writes in *Rules*.)

CIRCULATING THROUGH YOUR RADIO NONSTOP

Dressed for success, LL released *Radio*, which was also Def Jam's first full-length release, in 1985. An immediate success, the set was full of LL's aggressive, brag-filled raps and Rick Rubin's harsh and lean production. *Radio*'s lead single, "I Can't Live Without My Radio," celebrated the boom box street craze and spawned a video that gave America its first glimpse of LL in action. The video was actually footage shot for the 1985 hip-hop film *Krush Groove*, which marked the rapper's first film appearance. *Radio*, which quickly was certified platinum by the Recording Industry Association of America (RIAA), also featured

Kurtis Blow was hip-hop's first major celebrity. A break-dancer and DJ before he became a rapper, Blow blazed an impressive trail for future rappers. He was the first rapper to land a recording contract on a major record label, headline a national tour, sign an endorsement deal, and sell more than 500,000 copies of a single. This image of him is a still from the movie *Krush Groove*.

the singles "I Can Give You More," "You'll Rock," and "Rock the Bells," a rough-edged party record based around a sample of hard-rock band AC/DC's "Let's Get It Up."

Not one to ever rest on his laurels, LL returned to the studio to record 1987's *Bigger and Deffer*. This time, instead of Rubin, Russell Simmons enlisted the little-known duo L.A. Posse for production duties. LL aimed the track "I'm Bad" at critics who thought his overnight success was a fluke. Though *Deffer* was characterized by such boastful raps, it was the first single, "I Need Love," that gave LL more success than he'd ever seen. Rising to number one on *Billboard*'s R&B singles chart, "I Need Love" pioneered the rap ballad. Yet, the song brought flak from critics who felt LL's soft touch was a disservice to rap.

But according to LL, he was just being honest in the song. Soon after it was made, LL met Simone Italia Johnson in Queens and immediately bonded with her. She was to become his first steady girlfriend, his future wife, the mother

of his four children, and, as LL relates in *Rules*, "the first woman [he] took [his] hat off in front of." Though they'd go through turbulent periods, in Simone, LL had found the love of his life.

LL was also basking in the affections of an adoring public. *Bigger and Deffer* was a double-platinum success that led to high-profile live appearances for LL. Alongside rap luminaries Public Enemy and the Beastie Boys, he headlined the Def Jam

LL Cool J poses with his wife, Simone (*center*), and his two oldest children, Najee (*left*) and Italia, at the world premiere of the movie *Enough* at the Loews Lincoln Square Theaters in New York City on May 21, 2002. He and Simone have two other children.

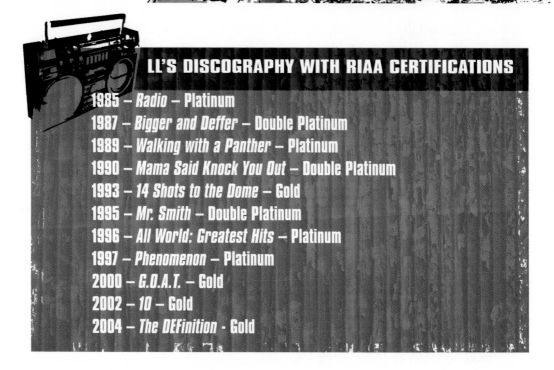

LL'S DISCOGRAPHY WITH RIAA CERTIFICATIONS

1985 – *Radio* – Platinum
1987 – *Bigger and Deffer* – Double Platinum
1989 – *Walking with a Panther* – Platinum
1990 – *Mama Said Knock You Out* – Double Platinum
1993 – *14 Shots to the Dome* – Gold
1995 – *Mr. Smith* – Double Platinum
1996 – *All World: Greatest Hits* – Platinum
1997 – *Phenomenon* – Platinum
2000 – *G.O.A.T.* – Gold
2002 – *10* – Gold
2004 – *The DEFinition* - Gold

'87 tour. He also became the first solo rapper to perform on *Saturday Night Live*. In 1988, LL headlined a Just Say No concert, reaffirming the antidrug message that he advocated in the video for "I'm Bad."

SWEAT, TEARS, AND BLOOD

Before 1987 was over, LL reteamed with Rick Rubin on the soundtrack to the movie *Less Than Zero*. LL's contribution, "Going Back to Cali," was another hit, going gold with the help

LL Cool J (center) poses with his DJ Cut Creator (*left*) and his sidekick E. Love backstage at the 1987 American Music Awards. LL was nominated for two awards in the Soul/Rhythm and Blues category: Favorite Male Artist and Favorite Album for *Bigger and Deffer*. In these still early days of hip-hop, Kangol hats and gold rope chains were prominent features of a rapper's dress code.

of its humorous video. The single's b-side, the scathing "Jack the Ripper," garnered just as much attention. It was LL's foray into battle rap, a stinging response to Kool Moe Dee. Kool had recorded the dis track "How Ya Like Me Now" for his 1987 album of the same name. Rappers use dis tracks to call out the shortcomings—usually the lack of skills—of one or more peers. This often results in a recorded response, or "answer record." On

CHAPTER THREE

DON'T CALL IT A COMEBACK

At age twenty, LL Cool J felt as if his professional life was already washed up, and his private life was no easier. In the spring of 1989, LL reunited with his father, whom he hadn't seen in sixteen years. Hired to be LL's manager, James Smith accompanied his son on the *Walking with a Panther* tour. LL considers the period surrounding this tour his lowest, most destructive point, in terms of his personal behavior. He had fled from the responsibility that the birth of his first child, son Najee Laurent Todd Eugene Smith, demanded. "It was a

shock to me," he recalled to VH1 in 2004. "I was like, 'Oh no I'm not gonna be young anymore, I have a son.'"

Feeling personal and career pressure, LL shared his fears with his grandmother. He told her he was worried that hip-hop no longer held a place for him. Her legendary reply ("Oh, baby, just knock them out!") provided the inspiration for the title track of his next album, *Mama Said Knock You Out.* Released in the summer of 1990, *Mama* found LL revitalized and as popular as ever. Esteemed producer Marley Marl, whom LL had met during a radio promotional appearance during the *Panther* era, produced most of the tracks on the album. In a 1991 *Rolling Stone* interview, LL described Marl as a "great acquisition." Marl gave *Mama* a more soulful feel than LL's previous outings, making good on LL's claim of being "the future of funk" on the set's first single, "The Boomin' System."

Mama Said Knock You Out yielded two gold singles: the smooth, midtempo ode to the girl next door, "Around the Way Girl," and the aggressive title track, which opened with the defiant line, "Don't call it a comeback!" The video for "Mama Said Knock You Out" is one of LL's most memorable videos. The MTV Video Music Award–winning clip spotlighted the hooded rapper training in a boxing ring and included a cameo from his grandmother. In a similarly aggressive form, another single "To Da Break of Dawn," took more verbal shots at Kool Moe Dee, among other rappers.

"I came out hard," wrote LL of the album in his autobiography. "Not gangsta, just hard." It proved to be a wise move, as the

LL Cool J strikes a triumphant pose after winning a Grammy award for "Mama Said Knock You Out" on February 25, 1992. He won a second Grammy in 1997.

album was certified double platinum and won him a Grammy for Best Rap Solo Performance for the title track. That song also served as the foundation for another career benchmark: LL's appearance as the first rapper on the MTV concert series *Unplugged*. The series spotlights musicians outside their normal context, playing acoustic instruments and recasting their songs in stripped-down arrangements. As an artist of hip-hop, a mostly electronic, sample-driven genre, the series posed a challenge that LL was more than willing to meet. With a full band behind him, he delivered a blistering performance of the song and showed the public that before anything else, hip-hop comes from the soul.

H.E.A.L.ING OTHERS

Riding high on the success of *Mama*, LL lent his voice to the Human Education Against Lies (H.E.A.L.) movement, a short-lived education advocacy program directed at youths that was founded by KRS-One of Boogie Down Productions. LL appeared on the single "H.E.A.L. Yourself," alongside Boogie Down

Productions, Queen Latifah, Run-D.M.C., Big Daddy Kane, and MC Lyte. LL broadened his civic outreach by forming Camp Cool J, a sleepaway camp for inner-city kids that emphasized leadership. He also became involved in Bill Clinton's presidential campaign and performed at his inaugural ball. (He would later also take part in Clinton's Americorps program.)

LL continued to dabble outside the realm of music with an endorsement deal for the urban apparel company FUBU. LL continued to publicly endorse FUBU for years, though his relationship with the company eventually soured when he sued it for inadequate compensation of work in early 2005.

This period also saw LL's first real acting roles, after cameos in *Krush Groove* and 1986's *Wildcats*. He starred alongside James Woods and Michael J. Fox as a detective in 1991's *The Hard Way*, and teamed with Robin Williams for the comic fantasy *Toys*.

SHOT DOWN

By the time *Toys* hit theaters in 1992, LL was already preparing his next album. Released in 1993, *14 Shots to the Dome* was widely considered a disappointment. During its creation, LL was plagued with personal problems. Estranged from Simone and his two children (Italia Anita Maria Smith, or "Tally," was born in 1990), he failed to find a true focus for the record. "It had taken me nearly seven years to get to the so-called top," LL wrote in his autobiography. "And it took less than a year to lose everything." *Dome* contained just one hit, the double-A-side single "Pink Cookies in a

This still from the movie *Toys* shows LL Cool J in his role as Captain Patrick Zevo, a man in charge of converting his family's toy factory into a weapons facility.

Plastic Bag Getting Crushed by Buildings"/"Back Seat," and became his first album to miss platinum status.

After some soul-searching, LL began getting his career back on track. His first step was to fire his manager father, whom he blames for the sluggish start of his film career (both *The Hard Way* and *Toys* were financial disappointments) and for the near loss of his house in Queens. (LL owed more than $2 million in back taxes, information his father kept from him until it was almost too late.) Also, LL entered a program to receive his high-school equivalency degree, or GED. He says that obtaining his GED was one of the smartest things he's ever done, as it allowed him to get a better grip on his business.

CALL IT A COMEBACK

Armed with that knowledge, he renegotiated his Def Jam deal and began managing himself with the help of Charles Fisher, LL's spiritual adviser whom he met through Russell Simmons at the start of his career. In 1995, LL headed back to the studio to work on *Dome*'s follow-up. LL enlisted a host of producers for the set, including Rashad Smith and Poke and Tone (aka Trackmasters). The result was *Mr. Smith*, a double-platinum smash that spawned the hits "Hey Lover" (a duet with Boyz II Men), "Doin' It" (a spunky romp with female rapper LeShaun), and "I Shot Ya." ("Call it a comeback, 'cause I'm tired of arguing," he told *Entertainment Weekly* in 1996, referencing the first line of "Mama Said Knock You Out.")

Mr. Smith came at a time when LL was maturing both as a person and an artist. (He told *Rolling Stone* in 1996 that the album was the first he made as a "grown man.") Even its cover showed a sign of change, sporting something previously unthinkable: LL's uncovered head. The album's content, too, was largely positive, with the romantic serenade "Hey Lover," which earned LL a second Grammy, and "Hip Hop," a love song to the genre. "My love affair with hip-hop'll never fade," LL raps on the track, which salutes a host of rap's heavyweights.

LL IN THE HOUSE

With his newfound maturity, LL was ready to take the plunge into married life. He wed Simone in a small ceremony at their Merrick, Long Island, home in the summer of 1995. At the time, Simone was eight months pregnant with their third child, Samaria Leah Wisdom Smith.

LL'S MAJOR FILM ROLES

1985 – *Krush Groove*	2000 – *Charlie's Angels*
1986 – *Wildcats*	2001 – *Kingdom Come*
1991 – *The Hard Way*	2002 – *Rollerball*
1992 – *Toys*	2003 – *Deliver Us From Eva*
1998 – *Caught Up*	*S.W.A.T.*
Woo	2005 – *Mindhunters*
Halloween: H₂O	*Slow Burn*
1999 – *Deep Blue Sea*	*Edison*
In Too Deep	
Any Given Sunday	

That year also brought a new facet to LL's career: he was hired to star in the NBC sitcom *In the House*, produced by music mogul Quincy Jones and Dave Salzman, the team behind another successful rapper-turned-TV star vehicle, *The Fresh Prince of Bel-Air. In the House* focused on the family life of a retired football star, played by LL. The show brought LL even more fame and taught him discipline he'd never before experienced as a recording artist.

Busy with his new stint on *In the House*, 1996 marked a relatively quiet year for LL on the music front. His sole output that year was *All World*, a greatest-hits compilation that contained fifteen previously released tracks and a remix of *Mr. Smith*'s

LL Cool J poses with costars Kim Wayans (*left*) and Robin Givens on the set of *In the House*, the television sitcom in which the rapper plays the starring role of Marion Hill, a retired football player who runs a rehabilitation center. LL won three Black Image awards for his role in the sitcom.

"Loungin'," featuring the girl group Total. *All World* scored LL yet another platinum certification. He hit the road alongside R. Kelly for the Top Secret tour. In addition to the arenas the tour hit, LL took the opportunity to perform some community work and visited hospitals, churches, and schools. He also visited the White House for the president's Summit for America's Future. He again was involved in voting advocacy through the Political Power for Youth voter registration program.

CHAPTER FOUR

TOO LONG FOR A SONG, BUT PERFECT FOR A BOOK

After spending much of 1996 busy with his sit-com, his tour, and his outreach initiatives, LL Cool J was ready to record a new album. *Phenomenon* hit stores in 1997 and along with LL's usual party tracks were "Candy," which detailed his relation-ship with Simone, and the intense single "Father," on which LL rapped about his biological father's absence from key periods of his life and the abuse he suffered at the hands of Roscoe. LL described *Phenomenon* as the "first-ever soundtrack to a book," and a month later, his soul-bearing memoir,

I Make My Own Rules, landed in bookstores. The book traces his rise to stardom and delves even deeper into his difficult childhood. "I feel you can't really help the young people and help the kids unless you show them where you made mistakes and then corrected him [them]," LL told MTV in 1997 on his inspiration for releasing an autobiography. "If you just talk about all the good things happening in your life, the bridge becomes invisible because they don't know how to obtain those things without going through the troubled times."

That year, LL also signed more endorsement deals, appearing in ad campaigns for Coke and the Gap. But soon, a track from *Phenomenon*, the single "4, 3, 2, 1," came back to haunt him. That cut contained a verse in which LL dissed rookie rapper Canibus, one of the song's guests. The feud started in the recording studio, when LL felt that the reference to his microphone tattoo in Canibus's original verse was an insult. LL fired back with "The symbol on my arm is off limits to challengers/you hold the rusty swords, I swing the Excalibur." Feeling slighted, Canibus retaliated in 1998, with the single "Second Round Knockout," on which he blasted LL's sexy image and female following, threatening: "Now watch me rip the tat from your arm." Never one to back down from a fight, LL responded with "Return of Jack the Ripper." Canibus's producer Wyclef Jean, also a rapper, then jumped in with "What's Clef Got to Do with This." But by that time, the battle had already fizzled out and LL had once again held his own.

PEOPLE WANT MY VIBE

On the heels of this public feud, which LL credited as revitalizing his interest in hip-hop, the multimedia entertainer was ready to work on his next album. In the meantime, he increased his acting profile, appearing in 1998's *Woo* and the hit horror sequel *Halloween: H₂O*. The following year saw even bigger roles with the successful shark thriller *Deep Blue Sea* and the football drama *Any Given Sunday*, for which LL underwent intense physical training.

In 1999, LL also launched his Rock the Bells label imprint under Warner Brothers Records. The label released the soundtrack to *Deep Blue Sea*, featuring two LL cuts and the debut from R & B quartet AMyth. LL had high hopes for the group and executive produced its debut, *The World Is Ours*. However, AMyth failed to catch on among audiences and critics.

Unfazed, LL released the boldly titled *G.O.A.T.*, an acronym for "greatest of all time," in 2000. "For me, the title is an opportunity to talk about how long I've been doing this and the fact that I really feel like one of the greatest at what I do—as an artist and musician," LL told *Billboard* in 2000. The album, which went gold and landed LL on the top of the *Billboard* 200 album chart for the first time in his career, included singles "Imagine That," "Take It Off," and "You and Me." The album also featured a gaggle of guest stars, Snoop Dogg, Xzibit, Prodigy of Mobb Deep, Q-Tip, Method Man, and Redman. LL told *Rolling Stone*

In Oliver Stone's *Any Given Sunday*, LL Cool J plays a wide receiver on a mediocre football team. His character is upset that a new quarterback will reduce the number of plays in which he is involved and, consequently, threaten his endorsement deals.

he made the album to have fun, though along with the party cuts came socially conscious rhymes. "Can't Think" examines the struggle of life on the streets, while "Homicide" tells the tale of three of his friends who had succumbed to violence. The track included the controversial couplet, "I don't mean this in a disrespectful way/But Columbine happens in the ghetto every day," a reference to the much-covered massacre that took place at a Colorado high school in 1999.

LL continued addressing his concern for America's youth by once again participating in the Rap the Vote registration campaign. His fourth child, Nina Symone Beautiful Smith (named after his wife and the soul singer Nina Simone), was born in 2000, a year that also found LL making a cameo in the big-screen version of *Charlie's Angels*. He followed up in 2001 with a major role in the comedy *Kingdom Come*, in which he starred alongside Jada Pinkett-Smith, Whoopi Goldberg, Cedric the Entertainer, and Toni Braxton. That year, he was also honored by the National Association for the Advancement of Colored People (NAACP) with the Outstanding Hip-Hop/Rap Artist award at the Image Awards.

ANOTHER SIDE TO SHOW

In 2002, LL's children's book *And the Winner Is* hit stores as he was reaching a career milestone: the release of his tenth album, appropriately titled *10*. Super-producers the Neptunes handled a few of the tracks, including the first single, "Luv U Better," another of LL's patented hip-hop love ballads. In the wake of the September 11, 2001, terrorist attacks, LL told *Billboard* that he strove to make a positive album—"a record that makes you feel better after hearing it." One of the most uplifting tracks was "Big Mama (Unconditional Love)," dedicated to his grandmother, who died of cancer later that year. LL's grandmother had advised him throughout the creation of *10* (she suggested he make the album free of profanity, a first for the rapper). *10* earned LL yet another gold certification.

LL Cool J autographs his book *And the Winner Is* for a young fan during the *Read to Achieve* segment of the NBA All Star celebrations in Atlanta, Georgia, on February 8, 2003.

With the release of his tenth album, LL's contract with Def Jam was up. In 2003, the rapper announced that he would seek a new home for his music, after the label that he had been associated with for seventeen years balked at his request for $20 million to re-sign. But a month later, it was announced that LL would stay with Def Jam. Terms of the deal were not disclosed. However, LL later revealed that he came to own 100 percent of his publishing rights and catalog, something he never had before and a rarity in the recording industry.

LL Cool J gives the thumbs-up sign after ringing the opening bell at the New York Stock Exchange (NYSE) on July 7, 2003, in celebration of his re-signing with Def Jam Records. He is accompanied by NYSE CEO Richard Grasso (*left*) and Russell Simmons.

Though his superstardom was undeniable and his rap career outlasted virtually all of his contemporaries', there was one benchmark LL had not yet achieved: a number one on *Billboard*'s Hot 100 singles chart. That changed early in 2003, when LL topped the chart with his duet with Jennifer Lopez, "All I Have," which heavily sampled Debra and Ronnie Laws's 1981 R & B hit "Very Special." LL had met Jennifer Lopez backstage at VH1's Fashion Awards and, once in the studio with Lopez, wrote the song "on the spot," as he told *People* magazine in 2004. The result was the biggest hit of LL's nineteen-year recording career.

By this time, LL's lofty stature in the music industry was unquestioned. Accordingly, many people sought his opinions on a variety of issues related to the business. In 2003, the U.S. Senate invited the rapper to testify at a hearing on Internet music piracy, a subject that remains hotly discussed. LL took a stance against free online music trading. "If a contractor builds a building, should people be

LL Cool J electrifies the audience during a performance at the tenth annual music festival at the Superdome in New Orleans, Louisiana, on July 3, 2004. In an industry in which careers are short-lived, LL continues to woo audiences with his energetic raps after more than twenty years in the business.

allowed to move into it for free, just because he's successful?" he asked the committee. "Should they be able to live in this building for free? That's how I feel when I create an album or when I make a film and it's shooting around the planet for free."

DEFINITIVE COOL

After successful turns in the films *Deliver Us from Eva* and *S.W.A.T.*, and with a Male Star of Tomorrow Award from the

ShoWest film festival under his belt, LL filmed the thriller *Edison* with Kevin Spacey, Morgan Freeman, and Justin Timberlake. He also announced that he was starting his own clothing line, named James Todd Smith, and a film production company.

But despite his thriving career as an actor, LL is never far from the mic. In 2004, he released *The DEFinition*. The bulk of the record was produced by Timbaland, an innovative and successful hip-hop producer who has crafted hits for many artists. The album abounded with Timbaland's futuristic beats and marked a conscious change in LL's musical direction. Discussing

SELECTED AWARDS AND HONORS

1991 – MTV Video Music Award (Best Rap Video, "Mama Said Knock You Out")

1992 – Grammy (Best Rap Solo Performance, "Mama Said Knock You Out")

1996 – New York National Academy of Recording Arts and Sciences Hero Award

1997 – Rock the Vote's Patrick Lippert Award

1997 – MTV Video Music Award (The Video Vanguard Award for career achievement)

1997 – Grammy (Best Rap Solo Performance, "Hey Lover")

2001 – NAACP Image Award (Outstanding Hip-Hop/Rap Artist)

2003 – ShoWest's Male Star of Tomorrow Award

the rowdy first single, "Headsprung," LL told *Billboard* in 2004: "I wanted to come with something different. I didn't want to come with a ballad or a love song. I really wanted to approach this from a party point of view and really switch it up." Though club bangers dominated the set, LL hadn't sworn off romantic tunes entirely. The 7 Aurelius–produced "Hush" was the album's soothing second single. Its video clip featured LL's eldest child, Najee.

LL's most musically daring set yet, *DEFinition* was another gold success, the cap on the first twenty years as a hip-hop and pop music icon. A rap pioneer whose magnetic personality won him both musical and cinematic success, LL wasn't looking back on his first two decades as a star, but forward. "I'm an artist in the truest sense: from the heart," he told *Billboard*. "I'm not trying to keep up with anyone."

That attitude, combined with LL's work ethic and his unwillingness to stay down even when critics and audiences pronounced his career dead, is what has kept LL's career thriving and why he remains a consistently bankable star in the fickle field of rap. Whether in music, movies, or activism, LL Cool J refuses to be knocked down. And he may stay in the ring for good. As he told *People* in 2004, "Retiring is the furthest thing from my mind."

TIMELINE

1968 James Todd Smith is born.

1980 Smith raps for the first time in front of an audience.

1981 Smith dubs himself Ladies Love Cool James (later shortened to LL Cool J).

1984 LL Cool J's first single, "I Need a Beat," is released.

1985 LL Cool J's debut album, *Radio*, is Def Jam Records' first album release.

1987 LL Cool J is the first solo rapper to perform on *Saturday Night Live*.

1989 LL Cool J's first child, son Najee Laurent Todd Eugene Smith, is born.

1990 LL's first daughter, Italia Anita Maria, is born.

1991 LL appears on MTV's *Unplugged*, the first rapper to perform on MTV's seminal concert series; wins MTV Video Music Award.

1992 LL founds Camp Cool J; becomes FUBU model and spokesman; wins first Grammy.

1994 LL obtains GED.

1995 LL renegotiates Def Jam deal; begins four-year stint on the TV show *In the House*; marries Simone Italia Johnson. His third child, daughter Samaria Leah Wisdom Smith, is born.

1996 LL wins New York Academy of Recording Arts and Sciences Hero Award; is guest of White house at President's Summit for America's Future.

1997 LL's autobiography, *I Make My Own Rules,* hits bookstores. He wins MTV Music Awards' Video Vanguard Award; wins Rock the Vote's Patrick Lippert Award; wins second Grammy.

1999 LL executive produces AMyth's *The World Is Ours* album and releases it on his Rock the Bells imprint.

2000 LL hits number one on the *Billboard* 200 for the first time; releases his children's book *And the Winner Is*; participates in Mobilization for Education rally in New York. LL's fourth child, daughter Nina Symone Beautiful Smith, is born.

2001 LL wins an NAACP Image Award.

2003 LL hits number one on *Billboard*'s Hot 100 chart with "All I Have," a duet with Jennifer Lopez; wins ShoWest's Male Star of Tomorrow Award.

2004 LL announces clothing line and film production company.

GLOSSARY

advance The money a recording company gives an artist before his or her record is released.

answer record A song created to retaliate against another artist's musical attack.

battle rap An aspect of hip-hop in which two or more artists combat back and forth via their lyrics.

demo A tape or CD featuring rough, unpolished recordings that unsigned artists send to record executives, talent scouts, or other agents to drum up interest in their careers.

gold When used to describe recorded music, this signifies the shipment of 500,000 copies of the record, as certified by the Recording Industry Association of America (RIAA).

mixer An electronic device used to blend or cut between two audio sources.

platinum Used to describe the shipment of 1 million copies of a recorded release, as certified by the RIAA.

sample An existing sound (often taken from previously recorded music) used in a new recording.

sellout A term used to describe a hypocrite, or in music, someone willing to compromise their morals to sell records.

turntable A record player.

12" single A long-form, vinyl release of a song, often containing alternate versions and bonus tracks.

FOR MORE INFORMATION

Def Jam Records
Island Def Jam Group
825 Eighth Avenue, 28th Floor
New York, NY 10019
(212) 333-8000
Web site: http://www.defjam.com

Web Sites

Due to the changing nature of Internet links, the Rosen Publishing Group, Inc., has developed an online list of Web sites related to the subject of this book. This site is updated regularly. Please use this link to access the list:

http://www.rosenlinks.com/lhhb/llcj

FOR FURTHER READING

Bogdanov, Vladimir, Chris Woodstra, Stephen Thomas Erlewine, and John Bush, eds. *All Music Guide to Hip-Hop: The Definitive Guide to Rap and Hip-Hop.* San Francisco, CA: Backbeat Books, 2003.

Cooper, Martha, photographer. *Hip Hop Files: Photographs, 1979–1984.* New York, NY: From Here to Fame, 2004.

Fricke, Jim, and Charlie Ahearn, eds. *Yes, Yes Y'all: The Experience Music Project Oral History of Hip-Hop's First Decade.* Cambridge, MA: Da Capo Press, 2002.

Light, Alan, ed. *The Vibe History of Hip-Hop.* New York, NY: Three Rivers Press, 1999.

Smith, James Todd, and Karen Hunter. *I Make My Own Rules.* New York, NY: St. Martin's Press, 1997.

BIBLIOGRAPHY

Behind the Music: LL Cool J. Produced by Brad Bernstein. VH1, 1994.

Brewster, Bill, and Frank Broughton. *Last Night a DJ Saved My Life*. New York, NY: Grove Press, 1999.

Chappell, Kevin. "LL Cool J Turns Up the Heat and Talks About Love, Marriage and Why He Gave Up 'The Naked Look.'" *Ebony*, Vol. 53, No. 1, January 2003, pp. 116–120.

Jenkins, Sascha, Elliott Wilson, Chairman Mao, Gabriel Alvarez, and Brent Rollins. *Egotrip's Book of Rap Lists*. New York, NY: St. Martin's Griffin, 1999.

Simmons, Russell, and Nelson George. *Life and Def*. New York, NY: Random House, 2001.

Smith, James Todd, and Karen Hunter. *I Make My Own Rules* (Parental Advisory Edition). New York, NY: St. Martin's Press, 1997.

INDEX

About the Author

Rich Juzwiak lives in Brooklyn, New York, where he writes about all kinds of music, including hip-hop, for various publications. The first rap album he ever bought was LL Cool J's *Mama Said Knock You Out.* Like LL, Rich can't live without his radio.

Photo Credits

Designer: Thomas Forget
Editor: Wayne Anderson